OLD AUCHINLECK
by
Alex F. Young

Townfoot *circa* 1913, including Orchard Place named, possibly, for the stand of apple trees in Willie King's garden. Beyond the outside stairway, the line of washing indicates the break later opened to provide access to Currie's aerated water factory, on the site of which Tesco is now.

© Alex F. Young 2005
First published in the United Kingdom, 2005,
by Stenlake Publishing Ltd.
Telephone: 01290 551122
Printed by Cordfall Ltd., Glasgow, G21 2QA

ISBN 1 84033 337 5

**The publishers regret that they cannot supply
copies of any pictures featured in this book.**

FURTHER READING

The books listed below were used by the author during his research. None of them are available from Stenlake Publishing. Those interested in finding out more are advised to contact their local bookshop or reference library.

Auchinleck Memories, Auchinleck Living Memory Group, 1999
Auld Affleck, The History of Auchinleck, Auchinleck Living Memory Group, 2002
Ayrshire Miners' Rows, McKerrell and Brown, pub. AANHS 1979
Adam Wilson & Sons, The History of a Firm of Timber Merchants, pub. Adam Wilson & Sons, Ayr, 1980
The Statistical Account of Scotland, Vol. VI (Ayrshire), pub. EP Publishing Ltd., 1982
The New Statistical Account of Scotland, Vol. V, pub Wm. Blackwood & Sons, Edinburgh & London, 1845
The Third Statistical Account of Scotland, Strawhorn & Boyd, pub. Oliver & Boyd, Edinburgh, 1951
Chalmers, George, *Caledonia, A History of Caledonia*, pub. Alexander Gardner, Paisley, 1887
Ross, David, *Scottish Place Names*, pub. Birlinn, 2001

ACKNOWLEDGEMENTS

Thomas and Jean Allardyce; Rob Close; Billy Crawford; John Davidson; Anne Geddes, Baird Institute, Cumnock; David Gibson; Bill Gracie; John Kirkland; Gillian Lonergan, Archivist, Co-operative College, Manchester; Thomas and Catherine Milgrew; Brian Mitchell; Thomas Smith; John M Stewart; Ayr Carnegie Library; Scottish Catholic Archives, Edinburgh (Diocese of Galloway); Scottish Mining Museum, Newtongrange. For illustrations: the Baird Institute, Cumnock: 12, 13, 15, 16 (lower), 17, 18, 21, 28, 29, 35, 36, 43, 45; Thomas and Jean Allardyce: 8, 9, back cover; the *Cumnock Chronicle*: 25, 26; Jean Kennedy of Ayr: 24, 33 (lower), 38, 46 (lower).

INTRODUCTION

Auchinleck is said to derive its name from the Gaelic *achadh* (field) *na* (of the) *leac* (flat stones), and was known as *Auchinlec* as early as 1239. Chalmers, in his book *Caledonia* stated 'this name is sufficiently applicable to the place' and that 'The lands of Auchinleck were granted by the first Stewart to a vassal, who assumed from the place the local surname *Auchinleck*'. However compiling the parish entry for the *New Statistical Account* (1845), the Rev James Chrystal wrote; 'Whatever may be the origin of the name, there is certainly a great abundance of freestone in the parish, though not altogether of that description implied in the name'. There could then, be some doubt whether the name was taken by Stewart's vassal or brought with him.

Only with the arrival of the Boswells in 1504 can the history of the parish (and the village they would later lay out) become reliable. That year the barony of Auchinleck had been forfeited to the Crown and James IV granted it to his 'good and faithful servant', Thomas Boswell – a faithfulness that would later cost him his life at the Battle of Flodden.

In the early to mid 1700s the village would started to develop and grow under the hand of the Boswells – and transform barren moorland into a viable community. In 1755 the parish population was recorded as being 887, but by 1791 had fallen to 773 as the population drifted off to Muirkirk's Iron and Coal Tar Works and to Claude Alexander's cotton mill at Catrine, where the population mushroomed from 1,494 to 2,779. In nearby Cumnock in the same period the number of inhabitants had swelled from 1,336 in 1755 to 1,632 in 1792.

By 1831 Auchinleck's population had risen to 1,662, sixty or seventy of whom were employed in handloom-weaving and muslin flowering in their own homes doing work supplied by itinerant Glasgow agents. The craft of box-making from plane tree wood (originally snuff boxes but later ornamental boxes of souvenir ware generally known as Mauchline Ware) gave employment to a further sixty souls. This trade had originated in Laurencekirk (Kincardineshire) and came to Auchinleck by way of Cumnock. Rare pieces of Mauchline Ware are now keenly sought by collectors both here and in North America.

Writing in 1837's *New Statistical Account* about the mines and quarries of the parish, the Rev James Chrystal spoke of the red sandstone and lime quarries producing 5,000 carts per annum and about the two coal mines at Barglachan, both of which used steam engines working at a depth of thirty fathoms. The twenty-four men employed extracted 8,456 tons a year, selling at five shillings or thereabouts per ton. These early pits were worked out by the time High House Colliery went into production.

The soaring population of the parish was mainly housed in miners' rows around the area, such as Common where there were five hundred housed and Darnconner where there were four hundred. By 1881 the parish population was 6,681, over four times the 1831 total. More came with the building of the rows at High House between 1897 and 1906. The early years of the twentieth century saw the building of private houses from the top end of Main Street to Searle Terrace, and round into Sorn Road which would shortly afterwards be flanked by the miners' rows of Dalsalloch to the north and the Ayrshire County Council housing to the south. Between the wars the county council built 403 houses and, immediately after the Second World War, house-building resumed with the construction of a hundred prefabs.

The Nationalisation of the coal industry on 1 January 1947 brought much-needed investment and, with provisional estimates of a century's worth of coal still lying beneath the fields around the Barony, the future appeared to be assured. Adding to this hope was the building of the innovative Barony Power Station, designed to burn 150,000 tons of washed slurry per year into electricity. The power station was commissioned in October 1957 and its twin cooling towers, each two hundred feet high, dominated the Central Ayrshire landscape. However, as deep mining contracted so also did economic sources of coal slurry and inevitably the power station closed in 1982. Within a year the towers were history.

Auchinleck was coal – the closure of High House in 1983 and then Barony in 1989 almost wiped out Auchinleck's *raison d'être*. Visitors to the town in the 1990s described it as a throwback from twenty years before. The closure of Currie's completed the forlorn image, but with the opening of Tesco a flicker of life seemed to return. Although still hardly a rose, Auchinleck is slowly being reborn with the building of new Brookside type private developments and the main street has started to claw its way back from looking like a ghost town.

Opposite: Alexander Young (1875–1945) with his wife Mary (1878–1957) and their six year old son James (1909–1998) in the rear garden of the Eagle Inn, Main Street, around 1914. Born in the East Lothian mining community of Penston in 1875, Alex came to Rutherglen with his parents in the 1890s to find work in the new Clyde Valley steelworks. He met, and married Mary Clark Preston in Rutherglen's Rechabite Hall – what the officiating clergyman thought of him being a spirit salesman is not recorded. In 1914 he took over the Eagle Inn from Robert K Miller and remained 'mine host' until his retiral in 1935.

View across the town from High House bing sometime in the 1950s. Following the early, typical ribbon development on Main Street and out along the Mauchline Road this photograph shows that with the colliery restricting any development westwards, new local authority housing pushed to the east.

Located near Bridgend Garage, little remains of the once thriving Bridgend (corn) Mill. Possibly the earliest surviving record is a 1745 tack from James Boswell, granting George Sampson an 18 year lease of Auchinleck Mill. At some time in the 1800s the road to Cumnock, which crossed Auchinleck Burn at the mill, was realigned. A trade directory of 1867 shows Andrew Gibb as the miller, and the 1881 Census records his widow, 76 year old Jane Gibb living at the mill with her daughter, Margaret and son-in-law Joseph Smith, grain dealer. It is unclear exactly when the mill fell into disuse, but clearly was so by the time this picture was taken sometime around 1910.

Flanked by Mansfield View on the left and Woodlea Cottage to the right in this picture, is the Town Hall, or Victoria Hall – its earnest beginnings having started in Queen Victoria's Golden Jubilee year, 1887. From its opening on 24 August 1891, the hall was 'home' to local organisations and events from the Debating Society to the annual flower show and gave the village a focus. It remained the sole public hall until the opening of the new Community Centre in 1958, and only the Star of the West Social Club sustained it until the inevitable demolition in the mid 1970s.

Lower Town Foot in the early 1930s, photographed from the newly-built gas works manager's house. The Town Hall is up the street on the right, and where the trees are on the left was later Bridgend Garage and the Miners' Rescue Station. Founded in 1857, the Auchinleck Gas Light Co. Ltd. initially supplied only the lower part of the village with, as its name implies, gas lighting, but the upper part had to wait until 1910. Until his death in 1903, the gasmaker was Irish-born John Devine, then a 63 year old, who had come to Auchinleck from Glassford. His son, Hugh Devine, succeeded him until he moved to Lasswade in January 1919. Auchinleck only adopted the provision of the Burgh Police (Scotland) Act of 1892 (enforcing the numbering of houses) in October 1925, so previous to this houses and blocks of houses were known by name – hence in this stretch there were – Millview Cottage, Avondale Cottage, Broadlees Cottage, Glengowan Cottage and Woodlea Cottage.

Bridgend Garage in the early 1950s. Returning to Auchinleck from the Royal Air Force at the end of the Second World War, John Allardyce who had spent his war fuelling aircraft, bought the land from Adam Wardrop of Fore Rogerton Farm and started his engineering-cum-garage business. Over the years the emphasis has moved towards motor vehicles.

Under the headline 'The Grocer Drops In', Bill Aitken of the *Cumnock Chronicle*, seen here wearing the soft hat, was on hand to report the drama of grocer John Stewart driving down Main Street on his way to Logan Toll in January 1960, when Duncan of Cronberry's coal lorry swung out and into his path. Swerving, John missed the lorry and the bus stop pole but more especially the hedge fronting John Allardyce's newly built house, which might have saved him from overturning had it not been removed the previous weekend. Built on an Austin ambulance chassis, John's travelling shop took to the road in 1950 and was finally sold to Bill Withers of Lugar in 1978. Standing with Bill Aitken are John Allardyce and his son Tom (and the dog Dinky) whilst Mrs Helen Allardyce and Mrs Murray watch from the safety of the house. Bill later became editor of the *Cumnock Chronicle*. He was killed in a road accident in February 1980.

Past Bridgend Garage, the sweep of Main Street towards the cross roads at the Boswell Arms on the Coal Road corner. The cottages on the right survive, but the tenements beyond are standing in, what is now, Tesco's car park. Here once was Orchard Road with the slaughterhouse and the soft drinks factory started by John Davies of Kilmarnock which was taken over by John Smith and the McMichael Brothers (George, Jimmy and Bert) from New Cumnock, under the trade name of Currie's. Despite the Second World War and its restrictions on sugar supplies and fuel, over the thirty years from the late 1920s, Currie's were innovative with their products, ever increasing the range of drinks, lollipops, snowballs and more – and aggressive with their competitors, often buying them out to expand. In 1959 Bert, the sole surviving brother, retired and the business was sold to the Morton family (of BMK carpets). Business again flourished until the beginning of the 1990s when Dunn & Moore bought, firstly, the pub and beer trade and then, in 1993, the whole business, soon after which Auchinleck was abandoned. The site served as a small trading estate until bought by Tesco, whose supermarket opened in 2000.

The Miners' Rescue Station (or Life Saving Station as it was originally known) was built in 1913 on a 'garden' in lower Main Street owned by Alexander Gardiner, a mason, then living in South Africa. Following the enactment of the Mines Accidents (Rescue & Aid) (Scotland) Act of 1910, requiring mine owners to provide, and maintain rescue equipment and for employees to be trained in rescue and first aid, a body known as the Ayrshire Coalowners Association financed the building of the station. Jonathon Telfer was its first attendant-cum-ambulance-driver-cum-caretaker (and secretary of the Bowling Club) living in the upper storey until 1924 when he was succeeded by David Hunter. The ambulance was used for emergencies in the village.

St Patrick's football team outside Saint Patrick's Church at Birnieknowe around 1920–21. Front row (left to right): John Patrick, Ballochmyle Rows; Patrick Keirnan, Darnconner; Edward Scanlon, Birnieknowe; Canon Vignoles; Michael Hayes, Common Row; Frank Loy, Common Row; (?) Loy, Darnconner. Back row: (George?) Loy; John McCaig, Cronberry; Daniel Gilroy (from Cronberry, Dan worked as a handyman about the convent and church); John Devlin, Common Row; the Rev Letters; Robert Carroll, Common Row; Alan McCormack, Birnieknowe. The Very Rev Reginald Canon Vignoles was born 1863 in Cork, studied at Dublin and Paris, and came to Auchinleck in 1918. He retired, on ill-health, to Castle Douglas in 1930. Born at Stirling in 1854, the Rev Frederick Letters was ordained at Glasgow in 1877 and came from Irvine to Auchinleck in 1915, retiring in 1926. Of the lads who did not follow their fathers underground, John Devlin emigrated to America's Pittsburgh and Edward Scanlon joined the priesthood.

Home supporters on the terracing at Beechwood Park in the 1950s – and by the relaxed atmosphere, Cumnock were not the visitors. Named to honour Lord Talbot de Malahide, who granted the ground to the club free of charge, Auchinleck Talbot played its first game here in August 1909 and have been a formidable side over the years. Players have come and gone – but not the supporters, who, in this photograph include; Hughie Milne (first cap from the left), with Tom McIlwean behind him; to the right is Mrs Conchar with Bobby Queen at her right elbow; and John Herbertson, centre of the three lads in front.

Coal Road with its run of tenements on the left and the Boswell Arms and cottages on the right, running to Green Gates. Its name suggests early mining, and the 1856 Ordnance Survey map shows the Birnieknowe area strewn with 'Old Coal Pits'. The Boswell Arms dates from the 1760s when the shoemaker John Kay is said to have obtained a 999 year lease on the building. At the time of this photograph, around 1911, it was owned by William Morton, a wine merchant from Mount Florida (Glasgow). A patient horse is standing between the shafts of what appears to be a fruit and vegetable cart – perhaps Old Geordie Sloss was making a delivery to the Boswell Arms.

Church Hill, or Church Brae or Kirk Brae, photographed from Coal Road about 1910. On the left corner is Martin Cottage and on the right, Dunsyre, built in 1898 by Dr John Gilmour Kerr but then home to Dr Charles Stewart. The cottages on the right appear on the OS map of 1856, and the name of Alma Cottage, in the centre of the row, commemorates the first battle of the Crimean War on 20 September 1854 (when the British and French routed the Russians).

The parish church, photographed from the track leading to the manse. This was being built as the Rev James Chrystal was writing the Auchinleck Parish entry for the *New Statistical Account* in September 1837. With an ever growing congregation – services were being held in the churchyard – agreement was finally reached in 1836, between the Kirk Session, the Presbytery and the Boswell family as heritors, to build a new church. With a capacity upwards of 800, it was completed sometime in 1838 at a cost of £750.

The earliest known church in the parish, predating AD 900, measured 18' by 10', and was enlarged between 1145 and 1165 to dimensions of 35' by 18' by Walter Fitzalan, the first Steward of Scotland. In 1239 his grandson, also Walter Fitzalan, granted it to Paisley Abbey. In 1620 ownership passed to the Boswell family through marriage. Despite a 1643 act of the General Assembly of the Church of Scotland proscribing such, the Boswells continued to use the church as a crypt. With the building of the new church between 1836 and 1838, the roof was removed to avoid property taxes, and decay inevitably set in. This photograph shows what Gordon Hoyle, John Paterson and John McCulloch took on, when they founded the Auchinleck Boswell Society in January 1970 to restore the building as a monument and museum to the Boswell family.

By late 1971 they had restored the bell tower and raised the external walls to a height of twelve feet. In 1976, when the project came to the notice of the Manpower Services Commission, the Society was granted £22,000 and the facilities of Job Creation labour. A further £11,000 was found by Hoyle and his committee through the Boswell family and public appeals.

On 18 August 1979 the museum was opened by Lord Ross, a former Dean of the Faculty of Advocates recalling that Alexander Boswell, Lord Auchinleck (1706–82), had also been a member of that august body. This photograph shows the display cases (unfilled before the opening) and, on the west wall, the portraits of the Rev Dr James J Chrystal and his wife Sophia, flanking the window, and David Boswell and his wife Anne Hamilton to the left and Captain and Mrs Bruce Boswell to the right. Centre is the church bell and a bronze bust of James Boswell, man of letters and biographer of Dr Samuel Johnston. By the late 1990s interest in the museum had waned and in December 2004 the Auchinleck Boswell Society was wound up. The artefacts inside went to the Landmark Trust at Auchinleck House and the building was returned to East Ayrshire Council.

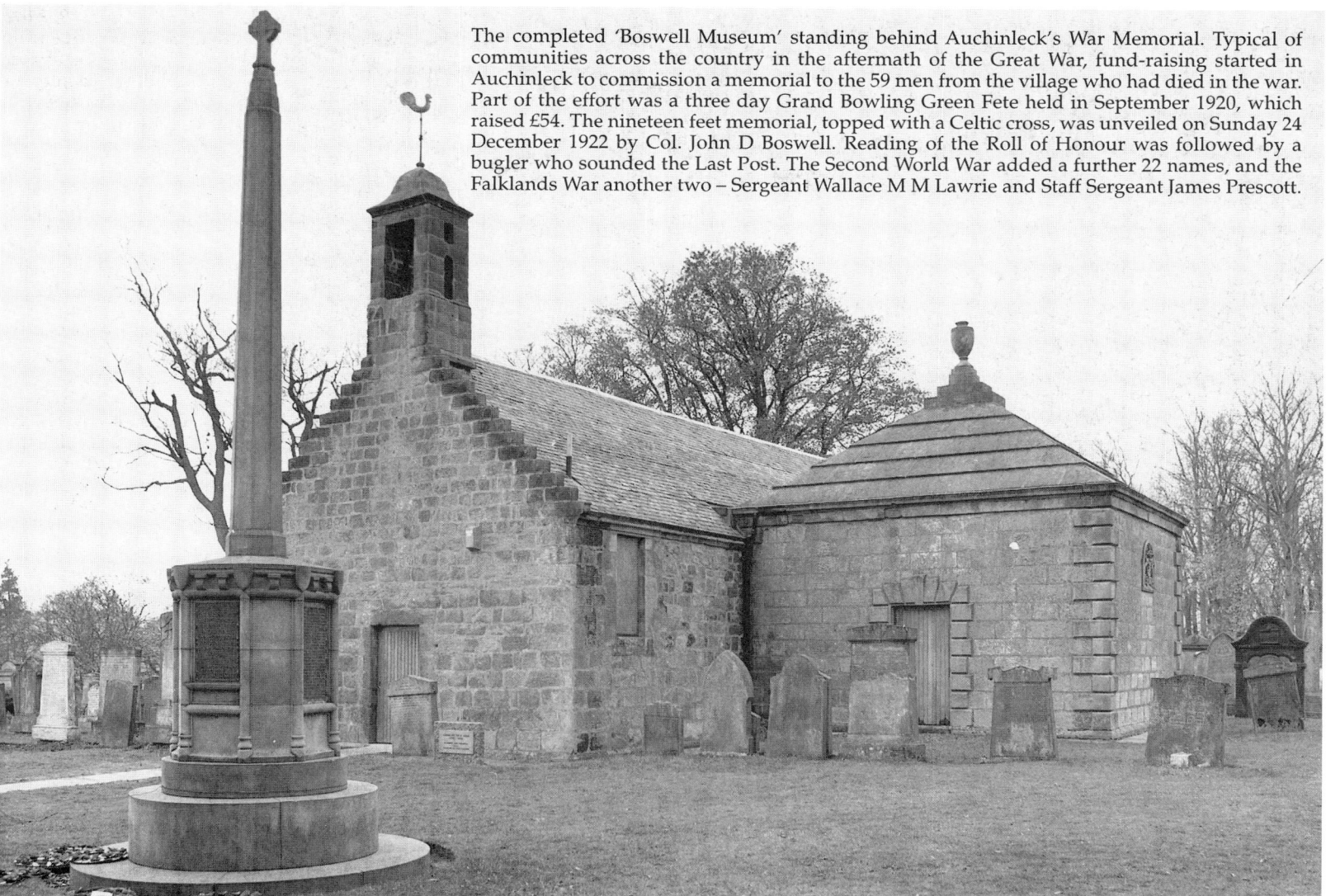

The completed 'Boswell Museum' standing behind Auchinleck's War Memorial. Typical of communities across the country in the aftermath of the Great War, fund-raising started in Auchinleck to commission a memorial to the 59 men from the village who had died in the war. Part of the effort was a three day Grand Bowling Green Fete held in September 1920, which raised £54. The nineteen feet memorial, topped with a Celtic cross, was unveiled on Sunday 24 December 1922 by Col. John D Boswell. Reading of the Roll of Honour was followed by a bugler who sounded the Last Post. The Second World War added a further 22 names, and the Falklands War another two – Sergeant Wallace M M Lawrie and Staff Sergeant James Prescott.

Work on High House Coal Pit began around 1898. The pit took its name from High House Farm, on whose ten acres of land it was sited, with headsman Andrew Steele and his wife Mary living for a time in the farmhouse. This photograph dates from 1904. In comparison to the nearby Barony, where men were working at 341 fathoms, the two shafts at High House were barely under the surface – 97 fathoms (582 feet) and 95 fathoms (570 feet). From them, four faces were worked; Ell, Major, Main and 40 Fathom, which by the 1940s were producing 185,000 tons of saleable household coal per annum by a workforce of 473 (369 underground and 104 on the surface). Following the closure of the pit in 1983 the site was cleared, leaving the left hand head frame and its winding gear in the shed below.

This 1909 view from the sma' bing, and across the railway line running from the colliery, shows the two parallel lines of High House Rows sweeping up the hill south west of Barony Road. The stone built row on the right, nos. 1–26 (25 and 26 having three apartments) were built in 1897–98, probably by Baird's own workforce, and followed by the 28 house, brick built, 2nd Row (nos. 27–54) in 1900, on the left. To the north end of it the 3rd Row, of 20 houses, and the 22 house 4th Row (starting with two, three apartment houses) went up in 1905–06. The rent for the two apartment houses was 2/1*d*. per week, and for the three apartment houses, 3/6*d*. per week.

Beyond High House Rows and the dog-leg on Barony Road, Hill Cottage, with its corrugated iron roof, stood alone by the roadside for many years. This photograph, from the early 1940s, shows the beginning of the area's housing development.

Barony Road, looking east towards Auchinleck, with the eighteenth century Glenhead Tollhouse on the left and, some fifty yards beyond, on the right, Glenside Farm road end. The 1881 Census shows the toll house occupied by Cumnock born, Miss Agnes Smith a 72 year old Toll Keeper (then redundant with the repeal of the toll road acts). Thirty years earlier her widowed mother, 73 year old Mary Smith, from Ochiltree, held the post. By 1902 it had been renamed Glenhead Cottage and housed two families; William Eadie, his wife Maggie and their five children, and, railway porter James Kilpatrick (or Kirkpatrick) and his wife Marion. By the early 1920s the building had become a garage or store, and it was demolished in the 1930s.

Work on the sinking of the Barony Colliery's two shafts, photographed here around 1915, was begun by William Baird & Company in 1906 to tap into the Productive Coal Measures Group seam. In February 1912 one shaft reached the Ell coal at 187 fathoms (1122 feet) and by mid May that same year, Maid coal was attained at 341 fathoms (2046 feet) in the other – making it then Scotland's deepest mine. There were many strata faults. Using longwall advance, the coal was brought out in 11 cwt tubs by slow moving, under-rope, endless haulage. In 1938 work began on a third shaft which would raise production from 1,500 tons to 2,500 tons per day. The work stopped in 1940, at a depth of 90 feet, and was not resumed until 1947, when it took a further three years to complete. The field was then estimated to hold 107,000,000 tons of coal, and at an extraction rate of 3,500 tons per day, to last for 100 years. The National Coal Board was created on 1 January 1947 and their report on the Barony, dated August 1948, shows the workforce to have been 1,264 (963 underground and 301 surface) producing 1,520 tons of saleable household coal per day. Production ceased in 1989.

The Barony Memorial, under the shadow of the surviving 'A' frame, on Barony Road. Missing from the immediate vicinity of the Barony Colliery were the usual miners' rows. Baird & Co. decided to house the workforce away from the pit and built 136 houses at Dalsalloch Rows, beginning in September 1913. Findlay of Mauchline did the joinery work, Ballantyne of Ayr the slating, and Kerr of Maybole the plastering.

The Clydesdale & North of Scotland Bank on Cowan Place in the 1960s. A century earlier, they had a branch in Cumnock, later coming to Auchinleck, and renting the shop at 180 Main Street from the fruiterer, Janet Ewing. In September 1925, they bought the Cowan Place property, then partly occupied by the draper Thomas Couperthwaite and consisting of three shops and dwelling-houses above. Although advertised as modern and commodious, the building required considerable work to convert it to a bank but, on 3 June 1927, the *Cumnock Chronicle* reported that the new branch '... is of roomy proportions and is fitted up with all the modern ideas. Two telling boxes have been installed and there is a cosy room for the agent [Charles N Morton] and a well built strong room'.

Auchinleck Co-operative Society's premises on Main Street in the early 1920s. With co-op societies springing up across the country in the nineteenth century there were several unsuccessful attempts to bring the concept's benefits to Auchinleck – both Catrine and Mauchline refused to open branches. Finally, at a meeting in the Railway Inn Hall on 19 December 1889, 25 of the meagre gathering offered their support. A room and kitchen on Main Street was taken on a five year lease, at £13 per annum, and opened for business on 25 June 1890. Sales for the first quarter reached £930 and paid a dividend of 2/3 per £. The adjoining room and kitchen was leased, and sales of £1,677 were realised in the second quarter – paying a 'divi' of 2/8 per £ to the membership of 190. Future growth and expansion was assured.

Possibly to counter what was becoming a bad trading year for Auchinleck Co-op, this 'Transport Parade' was organised by Mr James Morrison, the society's Managing Secretary (appointed 1915), on the afternoon of Wednesday 25 April 1932. The nine horse drawn vans and eight motor vans being decorated to represent the Society's furniture, tea room, bakery, drapery and clothing, and grocery and butchery departments, are seen here (and following page) leaving for Cumnock (the old Cumnock Society had joined Auchinleck in 1927). Creating great interest in Cumnock, the horse drawn vehicles turned for home, leaving the motor vehicles to head for Ochiltree (branch opened 1899) and the return to Auchinleck along Barony Road.

The society's vehicles had been in the news in November 1926 when a fire at their Toll Branch Garage destroyed two Vulcan vans, a Vim motor van and a light Ford van, but all were replaced with a new fleet of Dodge vans within 10 days. In 1940, the society celebrated its Golden Jubilee. A commemorative tea caddy tin was produced illustrated with photos of the three branches, the Manager and the President. By this time the society had annual sales of £175,000, capital of £84,710 and 3,058 members.

Main Street in spring 1906 when the Commercial Inn, still bearing the Cross Keys sign from an earlier time, and a few doors up from the Eagle Inn, was in the hands of Thomas M Pollock, the Cumnock spirit dealer. Before the decade was out he had sold it to Adam Ogg Brown of the County Hotel, Peebles. The delivery of coal on the roadway would have been for the baker, John Wyllie (now The Wee Bakery) and the Post Office, when Jane Crichton was postmistress. On the right was Mrs Ross's bakery and restaurant (selling tea and tobacco) and the entrance to Beechwood Square or 'Pole Square', then owned by Robert Barclay Waugh of Swansea.

Further along Main Street, where the writer of the postcard spent, 'my first 20 years', was George Maider, the stationer, the barber Richard Small and Thomas Steele the newsagent.

A parade coming down Main Street on a July afternoon in the 1920s. The Co-op buildings on the left included the Granite Arch Tearoom and its famous clock, mounted over the archway in October 1926. Seventy years later when the building was sold for demolition, the granite stone frontage blocks disappeared one Sunday morning and are thought to have gone to Ireland.

Built by the railway contractors Messrs King & Sands for the Glasgow, Paisley, Kilmarnock & Ayr Railway Company, the 'Cumnock Extension Line' – through Auchinleck – opened on 9 August 1848. In the days when railways were commercially driven, the new line was not only another step towards Carlisle – and the lucrative business to the south – but drove through the potentially rich Ayrshire ironstone and coal fields. At first, passenger services were sparse; from Kilmarnock at 9.05 a.m., 3.05 p.m. and 8.05 p.m. with return services, out of Muirkirk, at 6.45 a.m., 1.00 p.m. and 5.45 p.m. Like towns and villages across the country, Auchinleck was suddenly torn out of its isolation. The railway became a major employer; the 1881 Census shows it having over fifty employees, including sixteen labourers, thirteen surfacemen, five pointsmen and three porters. Joseph Irvin was Station Master, his daughter Marion the booking clerk, another daughter Mary the telegraph clerk, and his nineteen year old son, Hugh, the goods clerk.

This picture shows the station and its staff in the mid 1920s. Seated centre, and surrounded by some of his staff, is the Station Master Wilkie. The station was closed on 6 December 1965, but reopened on 12 May 1984 in cut-price mode minus the station buildings and staff.

Main Street around 1911, with John Henry the Carriage Hirer of North Waggon, Park Road, on the right. On the left is one of the many Kennedy of Kilmarnock water pumps, outside Hopkins, the fruiterers shop.

Either Lugar or Cumnock Orange Lodge parading down Main Street, past Easton Place around 1910. They amalgamated in 1928, and, retaining Lugar's lodge number became Lugar & Cumnock 'Star of the West' Lodge, No. 244. Venues around the area were used for their meetings, including Auchinleck's Town Hall. Only in 2004 did Auchinleck have its own Orange Lodge inaugurated, Brother James McCombe Memorial Lodge, No. 205. The shop with the sunshade was the milliner's, Maggie Dalziel who traded until the late 1930s. To its right grocer Gilbert Craig who in 1909 took over from James Nairn Gairdner, for whom he might have previously worked. He was gone by 1911 when the shop was the premises of David Arthur, the saddler. Easton Place was demolished in 1967.

David Campbell of Auchinleck Curling Club and his sweepers on Merlin Loch after winning the Lady Boswell Salver on Tuesday 5 February 1907. Of the seven first round qualifiers from the Saturday, played on poor ice, four had won the trophy on two previous occasions – a third triumph would win the prize outright. In the semi-final, David Campbell won easily against Hugh Alexander, whilst M Hamilton beat D McLeod by a single point. The following day two Auchinleck teams, were at the Eglinton Cup tournament at New Farm Loch, Kilmarnock. The 1856 Ordnance Survey map shows Merlin Loch in the north west quadrant formed by Market Place (then named Fair Ground) and the railway line, taking its name from Merlinhall on Barony Road where the High House Rows were later built. The Club's inaugural meeting was held at the Loch on 30 December 1861. Initially, membership was restricted to employees of the Auchinleck Estate and Lady Jessie-Jane Boswell gifted a silver box as their trophy. Three years later the trophy was the plate shown in this photography and membership was open to all in the parish. As the years passed, interest in curling waned. At a meeting in the Market Inn on 3 November 1946 the club was wound up – the Talbot Cup and the Howatson Cup and Medal going to the Bowling Club and a cash balance of £3. 0s. 2d. being gifted to the Auld Folks Cabin.

Auchinleck Bowling Club's Green around 1912. From around 1890 efforts were made to form a village bowling club – there would have been strong recreational competition from quoiting and curling – and find a suitable site, but not until 1901 was the club formed and, eventually, this site found. The pavilion was built and the 42 yard square 'Cumbrian Turf' green laid, for its opening on 17 May 1902., under the charge of its first president, the wood merchant William Wilson.

The Public School on the west side of Main Street as it (the street) sweeps round to Searle Terrace and the Sorn Road junction. The *Statistical Account* of 1837 records 'the parish school and schoolhouse are well situate, being close by the village' – at that time the village was clustered around the Coal Road/Church Hill junction. The Education Act of 1872 introduced compulsory education for five to thirteen year olds and in 1879, with the school roll consisting of 144 boys and 71 girls, planning had started on much-needed extra accommodation. Ground to the rear was purchased from the Boswells and the new extension, housing an extra 151 pupils, was completed in 1882.

Opposite: The infant class at Auchinleck Parish School in 1916, photographed outside what later became the technical and domestic departments. The class consisted of, front row (left to right): Robert Chapman, Dalsalloch Row; unknown; Daniel Muir, Highhouse; unknown; Alex Concher, Montgomerie Place and John Arthur, Coal Road. Second row: James Herbertson, Highhouse; unknown; Elizabeth Frew, Michie Place; unknown; Hannah Colvin, Park Road; unknown; unknown; unknown; Christina Toole, Cowan Place; Agnes Hall, Dalsalloch Row and Carolina Conn, Dalsalloch Row; unknown and unknown. Third row: Robert (?); (?) McColm; Flora Gilmour, Highhouse; Daisy Kennedy, Glenshamrock Farm; Polly Fitch, Searle Terrace; Lizzie Cree, Dalsalloch Row; unknown; unknown; unknown; (?) Chapman, Dalsalloch Row; unknown and James Pooley, Brown's Buildings. Fourth row: George or William Carroll, Highhouse: unknown; unknown; Hugh Harper, Shiloh Terrace; John Auld, Main Street; James Young, Eagle Inn, Main Street; Miss Allen; (?) Fleming; Thomas Wilson, Templeton Place, John Liddle, Highhouse; Dixon Andrews, Dalsalloch Row; Thomas (?) and (?) Murdoch.

Little is known of the early history, or beginnings, of the Railway Hotel but the name has to be a clue. With its newly-built porch, partially covering the name, and stained glass window display for Aitken's 90/- Pale Ale, this photo of the Railway may date from the summer of 1906 – James Young of the Castle Inn, New Cumnock having bought the hotel that April from Miss Mary Milligan, daughter of Mrs Janet Milligan, who had owned it since coming to Auchinleck from Dumfriesshire in the 1870s.

Shiloh Terrace (built c.1900) – taking its name, perhaps, from 1 Samuel, 3;21; 'So the Lord continued to appear in Shiloh' – on the Sorn Road corner, and the adjoining Searle Terrace (c.1905). The terraces were built by mine manager John Wightman and his second wife English-born Annie Reyna Morris. They lived in one of the houses before moving to another new house – Sharon Elim – on Sorn Road. A native of Auchinleck, John spent time mining in South Africa. His first wife, 33 year old, Mary Arnott, died at Johannesburg in 1895. Despite having a sizeable business building and renting houses in Auchinleck, the couple retired to Hawthorn Cottage on Ochiltree's Manse Street (now Mauchline Road), where they ended their days.

Sorn Road from the Main Street junction, photographed around 1915. The Wightmans' house Sharon Elim on Sorn Road acquired new neighbours when, in June 1905, a Mr Steele of Manchester erected four semi-detached cottages – and in October the following year Mr David Scott had James Richmond, architect and Provost of Cumnock, build two cottages, also of Ballochmyle sandstone.

One of these policemen would have been the village bobby Constable William McIntosh, walking up Sorn Road towards Arran Drive in 1914. Although the Ayrshire Constabulary was founded in 1841, with fourteen constables under the command of Superintendent William Thomson, there would have been no police in Auchinleck until Cumnock Division was established in 1869, when the force had sixty men. Ayr Burgh Police (founded 1845) and Kilmarnock Burgh Police (1828) were separate forces until amalgamation with the county force in 1968. By 1914 the constables in the 188-strong force were paid £86 a year, with fourteen days annual leave and one rest day per month – if they performed their duties properly.

Lambfair Gardens, Auchinleck

Within weeks of the publication of the 1913 *Royal Commission on Housing in Scotland* report, with its damning evidence on the appalling conditions of miners' rows in Ayrshire, things moved quickly. In September, work started on 136 houses on ground between Mauchline Road and the north side of Sorn Road. The next phase (to be built on the opposite side of Sorn Road) was agreed in early October 1925, when tenders were invited for the building of 64 houses. By the end of that month the Cumnock builder, Campbell, had started on the sewers. The naming of the streets was left to the Parish Council – and a number of special meetings. Suggested names included Boswell Street, Wilson Street or Avenue, (for the wood merchant) and (William) Murdoch Street (after the inventor of gas lighting), but in the event became; School Road, Lambfair Gardens (Auchinleck's last Lambfair was August 1902) and Old Street – a bizarre choice of name for a new street.

School Road looking towards Sorn Road, with the school on the left and Heathfield Road and Lambfair Gardens going off to the right. The *Cumnock Chronicle* of 28 July 1926 reported that notices 'inviting tenancy' had been sent out, and a fortnight later, that applications 'were not pouring in'. With many of the future tenants of these houses coming from the 'Rows', the apparent tardiness may have stemmed from the very reason the rows were in such poor condition – job security. The strong debating position held by Councillor Villiers Stanley Stoner in the naming of these streets was remembered at the next phase, giving us Stoner Crescent.

Mauchline Road, from the Market Place and Sorn Road crossroads, around 1912. On the left corner was the old tollhouse, later rebuilt by the Co-op (now Liddell's Garage premises) and on the right Campbell Place. The terrace was owned by father and son, Thomas and John Campbell, stone masons, each having four houses.

These vignettes on a 1903 letterhead of the timber merchants Adam Wilson & Sons show their saw mills at Auchinleck and Troon. Born in Minishant in 1823, Adam Wilson passed through a number of trades before finding an interest in wood as a saw doctor with Troon Shipbuilding Company, and aged 33 years took on a small sawmill at Sorn. In 1876 the business moved to new and larger premises at Auchinleck, conveniently sited beside the railway in Market Place. Initially timber was bought from Auchinleck and Dumfries Estates but as their woodland thinned, the search spread wider. The opening of a new mill at Troon harbour in 1888 gave access to the rich woodland areas around the Clyde, and another sawmill at Dailly opened up south Ayrshire. Adam died in 1898, and following the death of his grandson William, who lived at Larchwood on Mauchline Road, in 1919 the company headquarters moved to Troon. The Auchinleck mill closed in 1928, and became Robertson the haulage contractor's depot until 1960 when the lorries were replaced by Liddell's buses.

Mauchline Road from the end of Campbell Place probably in the spring of 1906. Beyond the gates, the row of 1890s-built houses were Hamilton Cottage (Thomas Clark Hyslop, miner), semi-detached Maryfield Cottage (Neil McKinnon, retired gardener) and Villa (Alex Mitchell, clerk), Murray Cottage (John Dalziel, Registrar), and Crichton Lea Cottage (David Crichton, postmaster). The two women on the left have jugs in their hand, perhaps suggesting the man with the cart was the milkman.

Templetoun (or Templeton) Place, on the left side of Mauchline Road, looking towards Auchinleck. This *circa* 1904 photograph shows, on the left, the two cottages marked Templeton on the 1856 Ordnance Survey map, the track leading up to the vicinity of Dalsalloch Plantation (later, Powderhouse Road), a 'modern' tenement building and the cottages of Greenockmains Lodge. Speculation as to the derivation of these names(particularly Templeton) abounds. Almost all of the properties were owned by Matthew Taylor, the fireclay manufacturer of Highfield, Kilmarnock. The first cottage on the left was occupied by Ochiltree-born, stone breaker, John McAtee and his wife Marion. Next door lived the boot repairer, William Clark. Greenockmains Lodge burnt down around 1918–19. By 1992 these buildings were all gone.